Most known for its red light district, cannabis cafés and canals, Amsterdam is undergoing a transformation. Restorations of century-old buildings are met with pop up art exhibitions and experimental food stalls. The unburdened ... d and culturally diverse populati ... 'or creative and entrepreneurial  s including world famous arti ... dustry, and a beautiful network of ... isitors alike to shape and explore

CITIx60: Amsterdam explores the Dutch capital and the most populous city of the Netherlands in five aspects, covering architecture, art spaces, shops and markets, eating and entertainment. With expert advice from 60 stars of the city's creative scene, this book guides you to the real attractions of the city for an authentic taste of Amsterdam life.

Contents

Before You Go

BASIC INFO

Currency
Euro (EUR/€)
Exchange rate: €1 : $1.16

Time zone
GMT +1
DST +2

DST begins at 0200 (local time) on the last Sunday of March and ends at 0300 (local time) on the last Sunday of October.

Dialling
International calling: +31
Citywide: (0)20*

*Dial the seven-digit number within Amsterdam. Add (0) for calls made elsewhere within the Netherlands.

Weather (avg. temperature range)
Spring (late Mar–May): 3–16°C / 37–61°F
Summer (Jun–Aug): 10–20°C / 50–68°F
Autumn (Sep–Nov): 4–18°C / 39–64°F
Winter (Dec–Early Mar): 0–9°C / 32–48°F

USEFUL WEBSITES

GVB (Metro, tram & bus)
www.gvb.nl

EMERGENCY CALLS

Ambulance, fire or police
112

Emergency doctor's office (24hrs)
088 003 0600

Consulates
France   +31 (0)20 530 6969
Germany   +31 (0)20 574 7700
Japan   +31 (0)20 691 6921
UK   +31 (0)20 676 4343
US   +31 (0)20 575 5309

AIRPORT EXPRESS TRANSFER

Schiphol <–> Amsterdam Centraal (NS)
Day trains / Journey: every 15 mins / 15–18 mins
Night trains (0100–0545) / Journey: every 30–60 mins / 14–18 mins
One-way (1st/2nd class): €7/4.10
www.ns.nl

Schiphol <–> Busstation Elandsgracht (Bus 197)
Bus / Journey: every 15–17 mins (M–F), 30 mins (Sa–Su) / 28–35 mins
From Schiphol, Airport/Plaza – 0511–0027 (M–F), 0517–0028 (Sa–Su)
From Elandsgracht – 0459 daily, 0522–2358, 0018 (M–F), 0521–2338, 0021 (Sa), –2354, 0021 (Su)
One-way: €5.00
www.bus197.nl

PUBLIC TRANSPORT IN AMSTERDAM

Train
Tram
Metro
Ferry
Bike
Taxi

Means of payment
Chipkaart*
Credit card

*NS only admits OV-chipkaart check-in with sufficient credit for the boarding fare. Single-use chipkaarts allows one hour of unlimited travel. A €1 surcharge applies.

PUBLIC HOLIDAYS

January	1 New Year's Day
April	Good Friday, Easter Sunday, Easter Monday, 27 King's Day
May	5 Liberation Day, Ascension Day, Whit Sunday & Monday
December	25 Christmas Day, 26 Boxing Day

*Museums, galleries and shops are likely to be closed on King's Day and Christmas Day.

FESTIVALS / EVENTS

January
FashionWeek Amsterdam (also in July)
www.fashionweek.nl

February
Sonic Acts
www.sonicacts.com

March
5 Days Off
5daysoff.nl

April
DGTL Festival
dgtl.nl

June
Kunst RAI
www.kunstrai.nl
Vondelpark Open Lucht Theater
www.openluchttheater.nl

July
PITCH
pitchfestival.nl

August
Magneet Festival
www.magneetfestival.nl
Lowlands
lowlands.nl

September
Unseen Photo Fair
unseenamsterdam.com

October
Amsterdam Dance Event
www.amsterdam-dance-event.nl

November
Klik Amsterdam
www.klikamsterdam.nl
Hardhoofd Festival
hardhoofd.com

Event days vary by year. Please check for
updates online.

UNUSUAL OUTINGS

Guided tours at de Silodam
www.silodam.org/guided-tours

Planned or customised architecture walks
www.architour.nl

Street art hunting
streetartmuseumamsterdam.com/tour

Reypenaer Cheese Tasting Room
www.reypenaercheese.com

Heineken Experience
www.heineken.com

SMARTPHONE APP

Public transport in control
GVB app
9292ov app

Marijuana café locator
Greenmile

REGULAR EXPENSES

Domestic letters / international airmail
€1.28/2.1

To borrow washroom
€1

Gratuities
At restaurants: 5-10% for waitstaff
At hotels & railway stations: € 1@bag for the
porter
At cafés, bars or on licensed taxis: Round up to
the nearest Euro

Count to 10

What makes Amsterdam so special?
Illustrations by Guillaume Kashima aka Funny Fun

Amsterdam's constant desire to innovate leaves no shortage of cultural activities, delicious food and a vivacious nightlife. Choose to relax in a café, cycle through the museum quarter, or party all night long – the city has something for every pace and taste. Whether you are on a one-day stopover or a week-long stay, see what Amsterdam creatives consider essential to see, taste, read and take home from your trip.

1

Architecture

Bridge Olympic Stadium
by René van Zuuk Architects b.v.

Jan Schaefer Bridge
by VenhoevenCS

Silodam
by MVRDV architects

De Bazel
Karel de Bazel

National Maritime Museum
by Daniel Stalpaert

Rijksmuseum
Renovated by Cruz y Ortiz Arquitectos

Het Schip
by Michel de Klerk

Islamic Funeral Pavilion Amsterdam
by Atelier PUUUR

Moravian Church
by 70f Architecture

5

Dutch Designs

Small labels & handicrafts
Restored
restored.nl

Select vintage products
Six & Sons
www.sixandsons.com

Fashion to FRAME publications
FRAME Store
www.frameweb.com

Furniture & everyday project
Droog
www.droog.com

Sunglasses
Ace & Tate
www.aceandtate.com

Restored industrial products
Blom & Blom
www.blomandblom.com

6

Markets

Europe's largest outdoor flea market
IJ Hallen (#30)

Daily neighbourhood Market
Albert Cuypmarkt
albertcuypmarkt.nl

Traditional & creative
Pekmarkt
www.pekmarkt.nl

Antiques & curiosities
Antiekcentrum Amsterdam
www.antiekcentrumamsterdam.nl

Farmers market
Noordermarkt
www.boerenmarktamsterdam.nl

Multinational bargains
Dappermarkt
www.dappermarkt.nl

7

Nourishment

Kroket
Van Dobben
Korte Reguliersdwarsstraat 5-7-9, 1017 BH

Bitterballen with mustard
Kwekkeboom
www.kwekkeboom.nl

Kibbeling (Fried fish)
Volendammer vishandel 't Centrum
Haarlemmerdijk 4, 1013 JC

Tompoes
Any bakeries & big supermarkets

Apple pie
Winkel 43
www.winkel43.nl

Stroopwafels
Lindengracht Market

Cheesecakes & pastries
Bakery Holtkamp
www.patisserieholtkamp.nl

8

Craft Beer & Liquor

The Double IPA & ZATTE Beer
Brouwerij't Ij
www.brouwerijhetij.nl

Butcher's Tears Green Cap Beer
Butcher's Tears brewery
butchers-tears.com

Bols Genever (Gin)
House of Bols Cocktail &
Genever Experience
www.houseofbols.com/visit

Jenever (Juniper-flavoured Gin)
Wynand Fockink (#55)
www.wynand-fockink.nl

Mama or Gaia IPA
by Oedipus Bier
Oedipus
www.oedipusbrewing.com

9

Hip & Happening Areas

Jordaan
Great bars, art galleries & specialty shops

Indische Buurt
Startups, design shops, ethnic eateries and dedicated bakeries

De Pijp
Albert Cuypmarkt, The Heineken Experience & boutique cafés

De Baarsjes
Mercatorplein Square, Vondelpark, Rembrandtpark

De 9 Straatjes
Bakkerij Paul Année, old cinema & bookshop
www.de9straatjes.nl

Westerpark
Westergasfabriek, Sunday Market, greenery

10

Leisure

Visit Artis
Netherland's Oldest Zoo

Go for outdoor weed or more expensive hash
And start walking the city

Enjoy space & greenery
Flevopark

Tune in to Red Light Radio
Listen to the sound of Amsterdam

Sauna
Spa Zuiver
Koenenkade 8, 1081 KH

Bike / Stroll
Along the Canal

Private canal cruise
Slow solar-driven boat
www.boaty.nl
Electric boat
www.sloepdelen.nl

Icon Index

 Opening hours   Admission

 Address   Facebook

 Contact   Website

 Remarks

 Scan QR codes to access Google Maps and discover the area around each destination. Internet connection required.

60x60

60 Local Creatives x 60 Hotspots

From vast cityscapes to the tiniest glimpses of everyday exchange, there is much to provoke creative juices. 60x60 points you to 60 haunts where 60 arbiters of taste develop their nose for the good stuff.

Landmarks & Architecture — SPOTS · 01 – 12

Expressionist buildings, modernised museums, iconic bridges and new housing projects represents Amsterdam's éclat. Bikes are ideal for a full-day venture.

Cultural & Art Spaces — SPOTS · 13 – 24

As well as contemporary art, Amsterdam holds classic literary and theatrical works in high regard. From film to new acts to dance to opera, take in local culture at any point of the day.

Markets & Shops — SPOTS · 25 – 36

Jordaan and Indische Buurt are becoming hippies and yuppies' new retreats, but the allure of antique shops remains. Ultimate design inspirations are paramount in boutique bookshops.

Restaurants & Cafés — SPOTS · 37 – 48

Bons vivants of all kinds of diet: rejoice in the city's food range, often enhanced by storied settings and a sustainable approach. Don't leave town without trying a Dutch espresso.

Nightlife — SPOTS · 49 – 60

Local beer, an evening of nostalgic coin-operated game or a raw club night, take a pick. No-wild-peeing code ensures a great night out without clashing with the locals.

Landmarks & Architecture

Expressionist buildings, classic museums and modern housing

It's not just the apparent uniformity of traditional slim, three-storey canal houses that speak to an architectural style observed in Amsterdam. Monumental landmarks like the iconic Scheepvaarthuis (*Prins Hendrikkade 108-114, 1011 AK*) and many working-class housing estates and local government buildings also reflect the architectural movement of Amsterdam School expressionism. This style of architecture was born from the introduction of a city wide building code created to unify the aesthetic quality of Amsterdam. Read more about the movement at Het Schip (*Spaarndammerplantsoen 140, 1013 XT*), a former housing block, now the site of the Museum of the Amsterdam School style and see its visitor centre, De Dageraad (*#1*), one of the most iconic examples of this style.

Renaissance relics can be found all over the city, including 17th century windmills like De Otter (*Gillis van Ledenberchstraat 78, 1052 VK*) old churches such as Westerkerk (*Prinsengracht 281, 1016 GW*) and most famously Amsterdam's expansive canal network.

Amsterdam's more recent buildings show its resourcefulness in modern architecture. From Kraanspoor (*Kraanspoor, 1033 SE*), an old crane way turned office block, to the Silodam housing project (*Silodam 351, 1013 AW*), built using an old dam and grain silo, the designs of derelict industrial spaces honour heritage, making mixed use facilities fit for purpose in a unique, contemporary way.

Jarr Geerligs
Art director, designer & artist

Jarr Geerligs is a freelance art director, designer and social commentary artist. He initiated postersinamsterdam.com, a growing archive of posters published in town.

EYE
P.015

Thomas Vørding
Fashion photographer

Born and raised in Amsterdam, Vørding knows his way around the city. He's recently started his own gin label, Vørding's Gin whilst working as a fashion photographer.

PostPanic
Film production studio

Overlooking the IJ waterfront, PostPanic is a Dutch production company made up of a bunch of international people who excel in creating commercials and long format film.

De Dageraad
P.014

Lloyd Hotel
& Cultural
Embassy
P.018

Liesbet Bussche
Artist

A Belgian artist who lives and works in Amsterdam, I mostly make public art and contemporary jewellery. I'm a researcher for St Lucas University College of Art and Design Antwerp.

Openbare
Bibliotheek
Amsterdam
P.019

Europarking
P.020

Pepijn Zurburg & Richard van der Laken, *Founders, Designpolitie*

We're the co-founders of graphic design studio Design-politie, column "Gorilla" and graphic design conference "What Design Can Do". Both are a father of two.

Berndnaut Smilde
Visual Artist

Born in 1978 in Groningen, Smilde does installations, sculptures and photography. His work is exhibited across the Netherlands and overseassuch as Toronto, Paris and Dublin.

Stedelijk
Museum
P.021

Stephanie Akkaoui Hughes & Paul Hughes, *Architect & speaker*

AKKA Architects founder Stephanie fosters interactions through space, where Paul gives talks at the Creation of Knowledge. Stephanie also speaks at summits worldwide.

Borneo–Sporenburg
P.024

GANZ
Producer, DJ & musician

Dutchman Jordy Saämena aka GANZ is claiming its spot in Future Bass scene. Besides being a producer-songwriter, he also enjoys world-touring with his DJ and Live sets.

Roel Huisman
Industrial & interior designer

I design interior, theatre sets and everything that goes into them. I live with my family in Kattenburg, an old part of Amsterdam right next to the former harbour area.

Rijksmuseum
P.022

Amsterdam Centraal
P.025

Jair Straschnow
Designer & artist

Jair Straschnow lives and works in Amsterdam. He is an award-winning designer, maker, enthusiast drinker and still trying to make sense of it all.

REM Eiland
P.027

Woes van Haaften
Founder, New Window

Woes van Haaften edits and curates for New Window, an online platform and design label that gives insight into the background stories of artistic objects it carries.

Smel design & strategy
Multidisciplinary creative studio

Founded by Edgar Smaling and Carlo Elias, Smel adopts a hybrid approach on their business of making books, communication expressions, editorial design and special publications.

Gerrit Rietveld Academie
P.026

De Ceuvel
P.028

1 De Dageraad
Map E, P.106

A working-class housing complex now par-
tially repurposed as Museum Het Schip's visitor
centre, De Dageraad (the Dawn) remains a phe-
nomenal example of Amsterdam School style
of architecture and 20th century socialist's
attempts to create harmony between classes.
An antidote to dull public housing designs,
this icon for expressionist brick architecture
conceived by Michel de Klerk (1884–1923) and
Piet Kramer (1881–1961) is marked by a sculptural
facade, decorative masonry and wrought iron
features. Although a distance away, take time
to walk around the full site at Spaarndammer-
buurt, also by de Klerk.

🕐 1100–1700 (F–Su) 🏠 Burgemeester
Tellegenstraat 128, 1073 KG 📞 +31 (0)20 418 2885
🔗 hetschip.nl 🎫 Hourly guided tour: €7.50

"De Dageraad building complex is a pinnacle of the
Amsterdamse Stijl of architecture. Every time you
walk around it, you can see the love for creation in it."

– Jarr Geerligs

2 EYE

Map L, P.108

Drawing on the interplay between light, space and movements in movies, Vienna-based Delugan Meissl Associated Architects envisioned EYE an equally dynamic structure that visually morphs when observed from a different standpoint and time. Standing in stark contrast against the city's historical town across IJ, its extensive offering of films, quarterly exhibitions and year-round installations at the basement also makes it an unmissable stop. EYE is accessible by a free ferry runs 24/7 from the Central Station (#9).

🕐 Exhibition: 1100–1800 (Sa-Th), –2100 (F), except between exhibitions, Basement: 1000–1800 daily
💲 Exhibitions: €9/7.50/6.50
📍 IJpromenade 1, 1031 KT 📞 +31 (0)20 589 1400
🔗 www.eyefilm.nl 🖉 Non-cash payment only

"Built upon the concept of film as an illusion of light, space and movement, this structure creates a spatial experience with human motion."

– Thomas Vørding

3 Lloyd Hotel & Cultural Embassy
Map F, P.107

From luxury emigrant hotel to a prison to artist studios, the 1920s Lloyd Hotel has been given a new lease of life. Using eight years of time, art historian Otto Nan and curator Suzanne Oxenaar transformed the protected national monument into a fully operational hotel and "cultural embassy", through its diverse events. The current interior design, a collaboration between Dutch architects MVRDV and designers and artists, is modern and open, a distinct contrast the exterior of the hotel. To book your stay at the hotel, see the accommodation section of this guide.

🕐 *Showtime varies with programmes*
🏠 *Oostelijke Handelskade 34, 1019 BN*
📞 *+31 (0)20 561 3636* 🌐 *www.lloydhotel.com*
🔗 *One-hour guided tour: €14.5 up*

"This building reveals its strange history through its various architecture, artist installations and experiences."

– PostPanic

4 Openbare Bibliotheek Amsterdam

Map P, P.110

Only a 10-minute walk from Central Station is Amsterdam's public library, designed by Jo Coenen (1949-). The grey shell limestone building represents a contemporary, accessible space full of internet access points, unexpected objects, reference materials, a radio station, café and more. Pop by the children's section as it occasionally hosts exhibitions with drawings and illustrations from top book illustrators. After your visit follow the IJ riverbank to see 'The Muziekgebouw', housing projects and renovated warehouses.

🕙 1000–2200 daily
🏠 Oosterdokskade 143, 1011 DL
📞 +31 (0)20 523 0900   URL www.oba.nl

"*There are two low-budget restaurants with both nice terraces, although the top one wins with the view.*"

– Liesbet Bussche

5 Europarking
Map A, P.102

Constructed in the late 1960s, this seven-sto-
rey, 24-hour parking block designed by Zanstra,
Gmelig Meyling & De Clerq Zubli, provides
a mesmerizing sight. Often referred to as
Amsterdam's answer to the Guggenheim, the
purely commercial space is adamantly modern
with its reinforced concrete columns and floor
slabs and symmetrical form. The bottom floor
is reserved for buses and the remaining six are
connected to the street through double spiral
ramps. In 2002, ten containers on the ground
floor were designated to house the homeless
and one container to host Waterkant, a Surinamese café bar that's open late.

🕐 24 hrs
🏠 Marnixstraat 250, 1016 TL
URL www.q-park.nl

"It is really eighties. So, let's call it ugly. But in its ugliness, it is one of a kind."
– Pepijn Zurburg & Richard van der Laken, Designpolitie

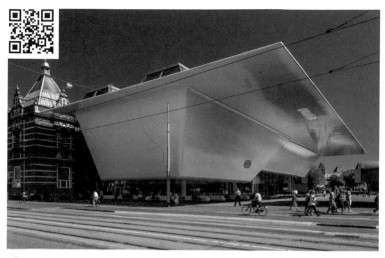

6 Stedelijk Museum
Map O, P.109

Stedelijk Museum, the largest museum for contemporary art in the Netherlands is a dichotomy between traditional and contemporary architecture. The original 19th century Neo-Renaissance brick building by Adriaan Willem Weissman (1858-1923) was given an extension in 2012 by a Dutch firm Benthem Crouwel, awarding it the name the "bathtub" for its deep white oblong shape. Conveniently located on Museumplein, combine your visit to the Van Gogh Museum and Rijksmuseum (#7).

🕐 1000-1800 (F-W), -2200 (Th) 💲 €15/7.50
🏠 Museumplein 10, 1071 DJ 📞 +31 (0)20 573 2911
🔗 www.stedelijk.nl 🖉 Free Sunday one-hour tours: 1415 (NL), 1545 (EN), Walk-in only

> "Amsterdam's best contemporary art museum and fantastic building."
>
> – Berndnaut Smilde

7 Rijksmuseum
Map O, P.109

One of the top 100 Dutch heritage sites, the Rijksmuseum (Dutch for "State Museum") is the Netherlands national museum of art and history with a collection of over one million objects. Recently restored from its 19th century grandeur after a ten-year transformation by architects Cruz y Ortiz, Van Hoogevest and Jean-Michel Wilmotte, the renovation highlights include the new Asian Pavillion, built from sandstone and glass and the 'outdoor gallery', a contemporary refresh of Pierre Cuyper's (1827–1921) original designs of a Dutch garden style featuring city gates and iron fences.

🕐 *0900–1700 daily* 💲 *€17.5*
🏠 *Museumstraat 1, 1071 XX* 📞 *+31 (0) 900 0745*
🔗 *www.rijksmuseum.nl* 🔗 *One-hour guided architectural tour: 1230 daily, €5*

"*This museum is once again at the cultural heart of the city and it is one of the few buildings in the world where you can cycle through. Enjoy the experience*"

– Stephanie Akkaoui Hughes & Paul Hughes

8 Borneo-Sporenburg
Map G, P.107

Amsterdam's eastern docklands region became a site for urban renewal in the 1990s, where many firms were commissioned to design elements of this mixed-use area. Rotterdam-based urban design and landscape architectural firm West 8 designed three iconic steel bridges that bring together the Borneo and Sporenberg peninsulas, and provide picturesque views of water. The variations in architecture, including de Architekten Cie's 'The Whale', which is an angular modernist building that redefines high density block design, make this former shipyard a mecca for urban architecture and a lesson in city planning.

🏠 *Borneo-Sporenburg, 1019 WZ*

"Take a walk along the various 'kades' (quays) and find how Amsterdam has turned its former harbour area into a paradise for architecture lovers."

– Roel Huisman

9 Amsterdam Centraal
Map B, P.105

Amsterdam's Central Station is the lifeline of the city, facilitating local, regional and international travel to thousands of people everyday. Designed by Pierre Cuypers (1827–1921), who also designed the original Rijksmuseum, this awe-inspiring gothic renaissance building has a cast iron roof and intricate decorative elements akin to a cathedral-like space with light illuminating through the ticket hall. The special pavilion in the east wing is reserved for the Queen's carriage. Although the public can't enter the pavilion, check out the beautiful gold ornamental gate that protects the area..

🕐 0500–0100 daily 🏠 Stationsplein 15, 1012 AB
🔗 amsterdamcentraal.nu
🔗 1–5am: enter through east entrance only

"From the station you've got a nice view on buildings built in old Amsterdam style."
– GANZ

10 Gerrit Rietveld Academie
Map U, P.111

Gerrit Rietveld Academie is home to the re-nowned Rietveld School of Art and Design. The school spans across two buildings: a Benthem Crouwel-designed glass-clad studio building, which opened in 2003, and the original build-ing, the Rietveld Building named after the late architect Gerrit Rietveld (1888–1965) who passed away during construction. Hailed as one of the greatest contemporary Dutch architects, Rietveld pioneered the De-Stijl/Bauhaus style of architecture emerging in Amsterdam in the early 1920s. This is evident in the Academie building with its rectilinear forms restraint in colour use and utilitarian design.

Frederik Roeskestraat 96, 1076 ED
+31 (0)20 571 1600
URL *www.gerritrietveldacademie.nl*

"The Rietveld Academie building is well worth a visit for architecture enthusiasts."
– Jair Straschnow

11 REM Eiland
Map Q, P.111

To get around Dutch laws that banned commercial television, REM Eiland was originally built as an artificial island in international waters of the North Sea in 1964. Authorities swiftly took control and it was destined for demolition but public pressure saved the historic platform, which has now turned into a restaurant. Climb up the outdoor stairs to reach the restaurant with the best view of the harbour. Concrete architects refurbished the space in 2007, ensuring the original spirit was maintained as an anti-establishment icon.

🕐 Lunch: 1200–, Dinner: 1700– daily
🏠 Haparandadam 45-2, 1013 AK
📞 + 31 (0)20 688 5501 URL www.remeiland.com
🖉 Non-cash payment only except gratuities

"REM Eiland is a good example of combining industrial architecture with hip and trendy dining. We love it."

– Smel design & strategy

12 De Ceuvel
Map T, P.111

Occupying nearly 4,000 sqm of a former contaminated shipyard in Amsterdam Noord, De Ceuvel is the city's first clean tech development site and a blueprint for urban development. Gifted by the Dutch government to a group of creatives, this spot has an open-minded atmosphere and is a great place to hang out in the sun, watch a movie or wander around the many refurbished houseboats. The newly opened crowdfunded bar and cafe serves honest, affordable vegetarian food made with imitation meat. De Ceuvel can be hard to find, so plan your route before setting off.

🏠 *Korte Papaverweg 2-6, 1032 KB*
URL *deceuvel.nl* 🖉 *Guided tour: €250 (up to 7 pax)*

"*A beautiful space, physically and mentally, for such an utopian project. It will definitely generate new insights and possibilities for the future. A necessity.*"

– Woes van Haaften, New Window

Cultural & Art Spaces

Historic collections, experimental creations, and national arts

A modest fee of around €50 can get you a Museum Kaart (annual pass) valid at virtually all museums and galleries in the Netherlands – a testament to the Dutch passion for enjoying cultural activities. Museumplein, the Museum quarter is a must see, home to Amsterdam's most important museums: the Stedelijk (#6), Rijksmuseum (#7) and Van Gogh Museum (*Paulus Potterstraat 7, 1071 CX*). An art lover's paradise, expect a constant stream of masterpieces by Rembrandt, Vermeer, Matisse, Pollock, Van Gogh and many more. Less than a ten-minute cycle ride away, peek into history at Anne Frank's House (*Prinsengracht 263–267, 1016 GV*) or find bright alternative inspiration at the Fluorescent Art Museum (*Tweede Leliedwarsstraat 5, 1015 TB*).

A new generation of cultural spaces has appeared, not limited to crowdfunded café art galleries, experimental theatres and DIY labs (#21). Amsterdam refuses to be siloed into categories. Every new space to emerge is multifaceted – NDSM Werf (#13) is a 'creative playground', and SSBA Salon (#24) is a 'cultural particle accelerator'. Visit a few of these ever-evolving spaces to witness innovation and originality. Carry cash on you as many of these places are so new they don't accept card yet.

Lex Pott
Industrial designer

An independent designer living in the Old South of Amsterdam and working in the North at NDSM-Werf. I work on both personal projects and commissions for labels and galleries.

Foam
P.035

Ronnie Besseling
Digital design director, Dawn

I love photography, good food, meeting new people and exploring new exciting stuff. Amsterdam is the perfect place for me to get lost in.

Remco Oude Alink
Senior graphic designer, Thonik

I am Remco (33), graphic designer and freelance DJ. I moved to Amsterdam eight years ago and love the mix of cultures in my neighbourhood Bos en Lommer.

NDSM-werf
P.034

De Appel Arts Centre
P.036

Aukje Dekker
Visual artist

I'm a visual artist and co-founder of Eddie the Eagle Museum in Amsterdam, which counterbalance the achievement-oriented art scene by focusing on subjects on the fringe of society.

Ons' Lieve Heer op Solder
P.039

INE & SANNE
Art director duo

Amsterdam-based directors INE & SANNE create an astonishing match between art, fashion and design in their art direction defined by a clean, strong and design-led aesthetic.

Bas Hendrikx
Curator

Born in 1986, Bas Hendrikx is a curator with articles published in magazines and exhibition catalogues about art. He is currently enrolled in De Appel arts centre's curatorial programme.

Eddie The Eagle Museum
P.038

P/////AKT
P.040

Dimitri Hekimian
Copywriter, SuperHeroes

I'm a French living in Amsterdam who work as a copywriter at SuperHeroes. In my spare time I enjoy endless picnics with friends, swimming in the ocean and writing.

Huis Marseille P.042

Philip Lüschen
Visual artist

Lüschen's works render the familiar strange. In a cartoonish style he visualises his scenario's using photography, film, spatial design and illustration.

Annegret Kellner
Artist, art blogger & curator

I left Germany to develop my career as an artist/blogger/curator in the Netherlands, with educational detours to Dresden, New York and Antwerp.

Athenaeum Boekhandel P.041

Mediamatic P.044

Mister Adam
Graphic designer

A.k.a. Adam Oostenbrink, Mister Adam is a (typo)graphic designer, teacher and creative factotum who works for international brands and cultural clients in Amsterdam.

De Nationale Opera & Ballet P.046

Petra van Roon
Founder, Barber Amsterdam

I'm Petra van Roon, living 50/50 in Amsterdam and Ibiza. I love creating in the broadest sense of the word: retail concepts, interiors, smaller craft projects.

Chris Julien
Partner, Novel

I'm cultural consultant and theorist based in Amsterdam for almost a decade. Also, DJ-ing at night, I love to bring together the heady thrills of high art with the seductions of city life.

Bijzondere Collecties P.045

SSBA Salon P.047

13 NDSM-werf
Map R, P.111

Set in a derelict shipyard is a creative play-ground, home to artists, designers, hotels, cafés and an indoor skate park. Visit one of the artists working in the Kunststad (Art City) or enjoy one of the summer festivals like theatre festival "Over het IJ". Once a month you can find vintage treasures at IJ Hallen (#30). Also located at the werf is architectural master-piece "Kraanspoor", an old concrete craneway dating back to 1952 ship building, now home to offices and studios with amazing views of the sky and the river IJ.

⏰ 24 hrs 💲 Ticket price varies with programme 🏠 Tt. Neveritaweg 61, 1033 WB
📞 +31 (0)20 493 1070 🔗 www.ndsm.nl
🔗 A free ferry journey from the Central Station takes 15 minutes and runs every 30 minutes

"You can see artists at work and it is located on the water so you are in the middle of Amsterdam but it feels like you are in a no mans land."

– Lex Pott

14 Foam
Map A, P.103

The Foam Museum of Photography is reputable for its choice to feature up-and-coming photographers and a diverse mix of genres spanning fine art, documentary, historical and applied photography. Located in Amsterdam's historic canal area, this majestic museum often collaborates with organisations to provide a fresh take on art, culture and photography. Pushing boundaries of social convention and creating new dialogues on a topic. Foam Editions, the museum's shop sells affordable limited-edition prints from both well-known and emerging new photographers.

🕐 1000–1800 (Sa–W), –2100 (Th–F) 💲 €10/7.50
🏠 Keizersgracht 609, 1017 DS
📞 +31 (0)20 551 6500 🔳 www.foam.org
🖉 Thursday free guided tour: 1830 (NL & EN)

"If you feel a little hangover and uninspired, go to Foam and you will feel inspired in no time."

– Ronnie Besseling, Dawn

15 De Appel Arts Centre
Map P, P.110

Inside this grand 18th century building you can find how young international curators and gallerists have trained to put theories into art shows. Currently directed by Lorenzo Benedetti, this non-profit arts centre also hosts a programme of lectures and performances by visual artists, choreographers, and theatre directors. Benedetti is known for his curatorial work for the Dutch Pavilion during Venice Art Biennale 2013. de Appels' library holds a huge collection of artists' monographs, professional literature, rare documentation and catalogues of exhibitions that had once been staged at the institution since its inception in 1975.

🕐 1100–1800 (Tu–Su except between exhibitions)
💲 €7/4.50 (excl. events)
🏠 Prins Hendrikkade 142, 1011 AT
📞 +31 (0)20 625 5651 URL www.deappel.nl
✐ 45-min guided tours: €75 (up to 18 pax). Cash and debit cards only.

"Expect condensed and heavy exhibitions in the spacious area at Amsterdam's docks."

– Remco Oude Alink, Thonik

16 Eddie The Eagle Museum
Map C, P.105

Created by an independent artist collective including Aukje Dekker, the Eddie The Eagle Museum places emphasis on talent - not age, medium or reputation. The subversive Museum has no fixed address and holds exhibitions, performances and installations that challenge convention and aim to surprise. Named after a former British skiier, Eddie Edwards who famously came last in the 1988 Winter Olympics and remains a symbol for 'the art of trying', expect the unexpected from this imaginative, collaborative crew. Check the website for programming before you go to find its current location.

🏠 Da Costakade 148, 1053 XC
📞 +31 (0)64 896 5406
URL www.eddietheeaglemuseum.com

"Eddie The Eagle Museum is my favourite. You never know what they are going to do or make. And, they preach art in its broadest form."

– Aukje Dekker

17 Ons' Lieve Heer op Solder
Map B, P.105

Formerly known as Museum Amstelkring, the Our Lord in the Attic Museum in red light district is one of Amsterdam's oldest museums set in a canal home. Built during the Reformation, a time when being a Catholic was illegal, the most special part of this space is the "*schuilkerk*", a clandestine church in the attic. Admire the ancient religious artefacts, a Baroque altar (c. 1715), church silverware and the collection of 17th century art. Remaining true to its original function, the Church still holds Mass, every first Sunday of the month at 11am.

🕐 1000–1700 (M–Sa), 1300– (Su & P.H.)
💶 €9/4.5 🏠 Oudezijds Voorburgwal 40, 1012 GE 📞 +31 (0)20 624 6604 🌐 www.opsolder.nl
🖋 Guided tours: €60 (up to 12 pax), 2-week advance booking required, excl. entrance fee

"*This museum really captures the spirit of the Golden Age of Amsterdam. Definitely worth a look!*"
– INE & SANNE

18 **P/////AKT**
Map D, P.105

P/////AKT is a contemporary art space in the east of Amsterdam. Serving as a platform for exceptional and emerging artists, the gallery presents large scale solo shows ranging in mediums and narrative. In addition to the public exhibition space, P/////AKT also has 12 creative studios. The neighbouring *Indische Buurt* (Indies Neighbourhood) is a rapidly gentrifying neighbourhood inhabited by immigrants, students and yuppies. Javastraat offers a mix of cheap fruits and vegetable stores, kebabhouses and start-up design and fashion stores. Don't miss Walters' bar at No.42 for a drink and bite.

🕐 1400-1800 (Th-Su except between exhibitions)
🏠 Zeeburgerpad 53, 1019 AB
📞 +31 (0)65 427 0879 📠 www.pakt.nu

"This cutting-edge art space presents large scale solo shows ideal for the more experiment-oriented audience."

– Bas Hendrikx

19 Athenaeum Boekhandel
Map A, P.103

In the heart of the city, the Anthenaeum Book-store is an Amsterdam institution. Occupying just 50 sqm, the shop stocks over 2,000 different magazines, ranging from fanzines and unusual one-off publications to international and independent publications – something for every taste and interest. It's also close to *Noordermarkt*, Amsterdam's most popular flea market where you'll always find a good bargain. If you love books more than mags, visit MENDO instead.

🕘 0930–1800 (Tu–W, Sa), 1100– (M), –2100 (Th), –1830 (F), 1200–1730 (Su) 🏠 Spui 14–16, 1012 XA
📞 +31 (0)20 514 1460 [URL] www.athenaeum.nl

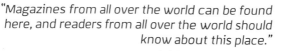

"*Magazines from all over the world can be found here, and readers from all over the world should know about this place.*"

– Dimitri Hekimian, SuperHeroes

 Huis Marseille
Map A, P.102

Set in a beautifully restored 17th Century canal home, Amsterdam's very first photography museum shows contemporary photography exhibitions from both local and international artists, changing every three months. Often described as having less "mainstream" exhibitions, the 13 exhibition spaces, photographic library and unique setting of the Huis Marseille offer an inviting experience featuring original buildings fittings, like fireplaces, a ceiling painting by Jacob de Wit (1695–1754) and restored floor finishings and light knobs. Don't miss the shop where you can purchase items related to a current exhibition.

🕐 1100–1800 (Tu–Su except between exhibitions)
💲 €8/4 🏠 Keizersgracht 401, 1016 EK
📞 +31 (0)20 531 8989 URL www.huismarseille.nl

"Apart from its high quality shows, the building and its garden is already worth the visit."

– Philip Lüschen

21 Mediamatic
Map P, P.110

Radical beer brewing, "Build your own 3D printer" and "An introduction to aquaponics" are just a few of the many workshops offered at Mediamatic, a collaborative art and technology lab. Pushing the boundaries of art and design through bio-based materials in inventive ways, the space aims to educate through workshops and exhibitions and incubate new ideas through its modern facilities. For an out of the ordinary educational experience, visit the lab. Book online in advance as the workshops fill up quickly.

⏱ 💲 Opening hours and ticket price vary with programmes 🏠 Dijksgracht 6, 1019 BS 📞 +31 (0)20 638 9901 URL www.mediamatic.net

"Exciting new site for an art, design and tech orientated lab where all the cool kids are."

– Annegret Kellner

The Special Collections of the University of Amsterdam is one of Europe's greatest heritage libraries. Founded as the City Library in 1578, highlights of the remarkable collection include early printed books (incunables) and medieval manuscripts like *Ethica* by Aristotles (1517). Whilst the collection's primary focus is education and research, it's also open to the general public. The Special Collections is now home to the famous fine Dutch bookstore, Nijhoff & Lee, a haven for any graphic designer. Tickets to the Special Collection are also valid at the Allard Pierson Museum.

🕐 1000–1700 (Tu–F), 1300– (Sa–Su)   💲 €7.50/3.75
🏠 Oude Turfmarkt 129, 1012 GC   ☎ +31 (0)20 525 7300   🔗 www.bijzonderecollecties.uva.nl
🖉 Guided tour: €75 (M–F), €85 (Sa–Su), max 15 pax

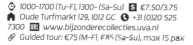

"*A hidden treasure!*"
– Mister Adam

23 De Nationale Opera & Ballet
Map A, P.103

Located on the shore of the River Amstel, the
Dutch National Opera and the Dutch National
Ballet share a custom-built performance space
that holds up to 1,600 visitors. The romantic
complex, nicknamed the "Stopera" took more
than 60 years to complete because of its
two-fold purpose as home to both stadhuis
(city hall) and the opera. Watch eloquently
choreographed ballet performances or experience the grandeur of the opera whilst enjoying
stunning views of the canals. Note that the
majority of opera performances are in Dutch.

🕐 Opens an hour prior to show. Box office:
1200–1800 (M–F), –1500 (Sa–Su) or until curtain-up
💲 Ticket price varies with programmes
🏠 Amstel 3, 1011 PN 📞 + 31 (0)20 551 1781
🔳 www.operaballet.nl

"Definitely check out the National Opera & Ballet
for the classical (as well as modern) and same for
music at the Concertgebouw (concertgebouw.nl)."

– Petra van Roon, Barber Amsterdam

24 SSBA Salon

Map A, P.102

With its online magazine, performance space and whole host of events, SSBA Salon connects Amsterdam's young creative class passionate about culture and innovative thinking, to the theatre. SSBA Salon's eclectic cultural programme is a mix of talk shows, exhibitions, and debates. There are no real rules at this creativity test bed, only high quality programmes and inspiring, forward looking ideas. Located at Leidseplein, relax at one of the large terraces of the bars around the square or grab a bite to eat from one of many food stalls.

🕓 24 hrs 🏠 Stadsschouwburg Amsterdam, Leidseplein 26, 1017 PT
📞 +31 (0)20 795 9970
URL ssba-salon.nl

"The 'cultural particle accelerator' of the monumental city theatre represents the city's new generation of culture lovers."

– Chris Julien, Novel

Markets & Shops

Local markets, local designs and local publications

Amsterdam is full of quaint shops, vintage markets and speciality items, something to satisfy every taste. When entering any shop, the expected Dutch etiquette is to greet the shopkeeper with a friendly 'hallo'.

If you're after a bargain, check out Europe's largest open air flea market IJ Hallen (#30), an oasis of preloved items that runs once a month at NDSM Werf. For something one-of-a-kind, pop in to any of the 70 antique shops near Museumplein. Since the Dutch are savvy and pragmatic you won't find a shortage of second hand or vintage goods. For the ultimate graphic design book store experience, spend hours in Nijhoff & Lee, housed in the Bijzondere Collecties (#22) or MENDO (*Berenstraat 11, 1016 GG*), an edgy bookstore with an intimate environment, packed full of creative titles and visual inspiration.

One of Amsterdam's most popular areas, Haarlemmerdijk is a long, trendy shopping street, stretching from east to west towards Central station. Emerging native Dutch brands by young designers exemplify Amsterdam's creativity. Check out Restored (*Haarlemmerdijk 39, 1013 KA*) which curates unique, handmade designs and LIKETHIS (#25), one of of Amsterdam's most coveted women's fashion labels and shops.

Frank de Ruwe
Founder, Natwerk

Frank de Ruwe is the founder and creative director of creative agency Natwerk.

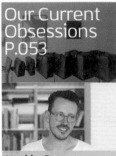

Our Current Obsessions
P.053

Noa Verhofstad
Photographer & set designer

Dutch photographer and set designer graduated Cum Laude from the Artez Institute of the Arts. Her devotion to staged photography is reflected in her work, are dramatic and surreal.

Joachim Baan
Creative director

Founder of Another Something & Company and Our Current Obsessions; co-owner of denim store Tenue de Nîmes and run a company that help building brands.

LIKETHIS
P.052

Hutspot
P.054

Bas Koopmans
Art director & designer, Baster

I am a graphic designer and art director running a small studio that mainly works for the cultural and creative field. I help organise Unfair Amsterdam, a local art fair for young artists.

Tenue de Nîmes
P.057

Justin Blyth
Creative director

Father, coffee lover, picture taker and art director from Los Angeles living in Amsterdam. I work on global ad campaigns at Anomaly and also publish my own magazine Iconograph.

Gijs Determeijer
Co-owner, 100% Halal

Hi, I co-run production and photo agency 100% Halal. I've lived in Amsterdam for 20 years. To me, it is really a cultural hotspot and a big village, which you can easily get around.

A Space Oddity
P.056

IJ Hallen
P.058

Ricardo Leite
Art director & graphic designer

Born in Portugal, Ricardo Leite works in Amsterdam on visual identity, editorial design and illustration among others within print and digital approaches.

David Douglas
Electronica producer

I make electronic music and released my debut album Moon Observations in May 2014. I also work as a video and film director, editor and make video installations.

Hedwig Heinsman
Co-founder, DUS

Co-founder of architecture office DUS. Their focus on unique design and innovation is portrayed by 3D Print Canal House project – affordable tailor-made architecture as a global housing solution.

Alex Kitain & Erica Armistead
Co-founders, The Coffeevine

Co-founders of The Coffeevine, a specialty coffee guide and delivery services. Hail from marketing and graphic design, great coffee and food is what they live for.

Gidi van Maarseveen & Adrian Woods, *Photography duo*

A photography duo who first met at the Royal Academy of Arts in The Hague. They mainly work on tangible still life and product photography in a playful and experimental approach.

concrete

concrete
Architectural associates

With a team of 40 multidisciplinary creatives, concrete develops concepts to help businesses and institutions on architecture, interior design, urban and brand development.

 25 LIKETHIS
Map B, P.104

Both a shop and a design studio, LIKETHIS was born from Fleur van Noesel and Urs Hasham's enthusiasm for fashion and is seen as a small revolution for the Dutch fashion scene. Inter-disciplinary collaborations form the foundation of this unique collection featuring clean cuts, bold prints, quirky styles and edgy timeless pieces, making it one of Amsterdam's coolest fashion brands. Although LIKETHIS only makes women's clothes, they stock items for men and stylish objects in their shop.

🕐 0900–1800 (M), 1100– (Th–Sa)
🏠 Westerstraat 70, 1015 ML
📞 +31 (0)20 626 1919 URL likethis.nl

"Make sure you check out the 'missing numbers' street art project in the small alley next door – between house number 54 and 70."

– Frank de Ruwe, Natwerk

26 Our Current Obsessions
Map P, P.110

Conceived by designer Joachim Baan, founder of Another Something & Co., Our Current Obsessions is a gallery, shop and Baan's studio in one. The space presents coveted brands in a vernacular borrowed from traditional art galleries with white walls and an abundance of space, which he co-runs with his photographer brother, Iwan. Baan's collection, born from his love of conserving things, lives online through insightful stories; and offline where you can browse the shop to see the full collection of curious objects. Near the shop is Waterlooplein where there's a daily flea market.

🕐 1000-1800 (Th-F), 1200-1700 (Sa)
🏠 Schippersgracht 7, 1011 TR
📞 +31 (0)61 506 0581
🔗 www.ourcurrentobsessions.com

"*Every three months the space is refreshed with a great curation of products and art works, from a cabinet of curiosities to books and accessories.*"

– Joachim Baan

 27 Hutspot
Map E, P.106

With its spaces divided between retail, art and food, Hutspot is a compact showcase of Amsterdam culture and definition of new urban lifestyle. Always wanting to be ahead of the curve, the shop unrelentingly seeks out new and interesting brands, products, designers, artists and entrepreneurs for modern kitchens, closets and bookshelves. Everything you find on site is available for purchase, so don't shy away from asking about prices. Their Van Woustraat café or Bar Hutspot is where you can stay for extended chats, live music and specialty beers.

 🕙 1000–1900 (M–Sa), 1200–1800 (Su)
🏠 Rozengracht 204–210, 1016 NL,
Van Woustraat 4, 1073 LL
📞 +31 (0)20 370 8708,
+31 (0)20 223 1331
🔗 www.hutspotamsterdam.com

 "It's a great place to get in contact with Dutch designers and artists. I'm sure you will get inspired when you enter Hutspot!"

– Noa Verhofstad

055

28 A Space Oddity
Map B, P.104

Whether you're a comic nerd, action figure collector or just plain curious, immerse yourself with pop-culture ephemera at a Space Oddity. Packed full of Marvel comics, manga figurines, He-man parts, Nintendo posters, Studio Ghibli plush toys and literally anything related to cartoons, animes and games, the tiny store has something for every pocket and person, regardless of age. If you can't find what you're looking for, it's very likely they'll be able to track it down for you. Go and spend hours surrounded by your favourite entertainment obsessions.

🕐 1100–1730 (Tu–F), 1015–1700 (Sa)
🏠 Prinsengracht 204, 1016 HD
📞 +31 (0)20 427 4036
URL www.spaceoddity.nl

"If you are a toy lover or just someone who likes odd shops, here is one you will love."

– Bas Koopmans, Baster

29 Tenue de Nîmes
Map A, P.102

Tenue de Nîmes is a connoisseur of great denim jeans, food, books and anything the founders Menno van Meurs and René Strolenberg consider "the good things in life". Creative partner Joachim Baan art-directed the store design, which now has three locations across the city. With an emphasis on function, heritage and quality of jeans, the stores carry a wide range of new and vintage denim. All staff are denim experts, so feel free to ask for some professional advice. They also sell limited-edition sneakers and run their own magazine, Journal de Nîmes.

🕐 1200–1800 (Su–M), 1000– (Tu–W, F–Sa), 1000–2000 (Th) 🏠 Haarlemmerstraat 92–94, 1013 EV, Elandsgracht 60, 1016 TX 📞 +31 (0)20 331 2778, +31 (0)20 320 4012 🔗 www.tenuedenimes.com

"This is one my favourite store to buy clothes, great selection of jeans, and work wear inspired clothes!"

– Gijs Determeijer, 100% Halal

30 IJ Hallen
Map R, P.111

Hosted in and around a shipping hanger at NDSM-werf (#13), the sheer scale of IJ Hallen alone is already a good enough reason to visit. Amsterdam's largest flea market offers the ultimate treasure trove of goods from ceramics, vintage clothing to objects you may have never seen before. Once a month (usually on the second weekend) locals and tourists visit the market to hunt for bargains from the rotating list of 750 vendors selling oddities from vintage bottle openers and analogue cameras to rags and rejects.

🕐 0900–1630 (Sa–Su, every three weeks) Ⓢ €5/2
🏠 Tt. Neveritaweg 15, 1033 WB
☎ +31 (0)22 958 1598
URL www.ijhallen.nl

"There are a bunch of great outdoor markets in Amsterdam. Some every day, some only on weekends. But IJ Hallen is the the best."

– Justin Blyth

31 San Serriffe
Map B, P.105

In the heart of the red light district lives this small art bookshop that has a vast selection of small press publishing, theoretical and artist books. Run by two former Rietveld students with impeccable taste and knowledge in graphic design, their books provide a rich experience to explore popular and unusual design topics, as well as rare publications and zines. They also run a weekly cultural programme of artist talks, book launches and exhibitions. The shop only opens three days a week and often closes for summer breaks in July and August.

🕐 1200–1900 (Th–Sa)
🏠 Sint Annenstraat 30, 1012 HE
URL www.san-serriffe.com

"Their stock manifest their faithful taste as well as a keen tip for a choice of subjects. And the best of all is their Thursday openings."

– Ricardo Leite

32 Concerto
Map A, P.103

Formed from a row of five adjoining buildings, this musical emporium is full of new and second hand vinyls, CDs and books across all genres of music from pop, rock, dance, metal, classical, blues, jazz. They also sell limited edition DVDs, posters and rare LPs. Among the row is Concerto Coffee where you can sample their music with coffee made from Single Estate beans and sandwiches or a flavoursome apple pie. Occasionally you might run into signings, film screenings, exhibitions and many live acts.

🕐 1000–1800 (M–W, Sa), –1900 (Th–F), 1200– (Su)
🏠 Utrechtsestraat 52–60, 1017 VP
📞 +31 (0)20 623 5228
🔗 www.concerto.nl

> *"The best way to start a day is by visiting Concerto and search a few hours for new interesting vinyls."*
> – David Douglas

33 Architectura & Natura
Map B, P.104

Occupying at the same address for more than 75 years, the small and cozy bookstore has proudly grown into one of Europe's best known booksellers and book press specialising in architecture, gardening and natural history. Their stock list features a magnificent collection of great classics and loads of new titles and magazines from their own press, as well as international and independent publishers in Europe and Japan. Don't refrain from adding your favourite books to your cart. Their friendly staff are happy to assist in making international shipping arrangements.

🕐 1200–1800 (M–Tu), 1030–1830 (W–Sa), 1300–1700 (Su)
🏠 Leliegracht 22, 1015 DG
📞 +31 (0)20 623 6186
URL www.architecturapublishers.nl

"Located on a lovely street. The pizza place next door, Da Portare Via, has good pizza that you can eat on the banks of the canal."

– Hedwig Heinsman, DUS

34 De Hallen Amsterdam
Map C, P.105

Restored in 2013, De Hallen is a complex of halls in an old tram depot housing tenants including a bike recycling workshop, a nursery, a library and many more community and retail spaces that promote social entrepreneurship and education. Check out the Denim Lab, a research facility focuses on the sustainability of the jean industry or get an edgy haircut at Kinki Academy, a hairdressing school. Each weekend De Hallen also hosts a local goods market, featuring a great selection of fashion and furniture designed and made in Amsterdam.

🕐 0700–2300 (M–F), –0300 (Sa–Su)
🏠 Hannie Dankbaar Passage 33, 1053 RT
📞 +31 (0)20 705 8164
🔗 www.dehallen-amsterdam.nl

"The whole area around it is brimming with new shops, a market, cute eateries and excellent coffee spots."
– Alex Kitain & Erica Armistead, The Coffeevine

35 Vlieger
Map A, P.103

With more than 140 years experience in paper and print, Vlieger is a family-run enterprise where you'll find a haberdashery of stationary, packaging materials and paper. From paper-thin silk paper made in Nepal and patterned French marble paper to stencil-dyed Japanese Katazome paper, explore the intricate patterns and weights tactually whilst learning about the origins of all paper from their knowledgeable staff. You can also find loads of art supplies including foam board, paint, lino cuts and many other things you didn't even know you wanted.

🕐 1200–1800 (M), 0900– (Tu–F),
1100–1730 (Sa) 🏠 Amstel 34, 1017 AB
📞 +31 (0)20 623 5834
URL www.vliegerpapier.nl

"The most amazing paper shop. They have hundreds of kinds of paper."
– Gidi van Maarseveen & Adrian Woods

36 zuiderMRKT
Map 0, P.109

The zuiderMRKT can be found every Saturday on the corner of Jacob Obrechtstraat and Johannes Verhulststraat in Amsterdam's South district. Truly a neighbourhood cooperative, the market buys fresh, organic fruits and vegetables at fair prices directly from rural farmers based on what's in season. Various types of stocks such as meat, bread, cheese, eggs, oils and other items are collectively decided by the 400 local members. Since the market only sells seasonal produce, expect a varied offering when you visit the market at different times of year.

🕙 0930–1700 (Sa)
🏠 Jacob Obrechtstraat 38, 1071 KG
📞 +31 (0)61 153 5521 URL www.zuidermrkt.nl

"Learn about delicious recipes, stories and forgotten vegetables at this nice food market where the neighbours meet."

– concrete

Restaurants & Cafés

Classical Dutch, nose-to-tail cuisine and distinctive veggie choices

Traditional Dutch food has a reputation of being stodgy and preserved – potatoes, pickled herring and salty liquorice. Don't let this put you off trying Dutch classics like *bitterballen* (deep fried veal balls covered with breadcrumbs) or raw herring (hold the fish by the tail and drop it into your mouth) available at many cafés and markets. The convergence of many nationalities in the Netherlands and its colonial history influences the range of food available and the fusion of flavours. Amsterdam has an abundance of North African tagines, Indonesian curries and Surinamese breads.

Plan a visit to at least one avant-garde Dutch establishment like Rijsel (#40) or Wilde Zwijnen (#41) where an emphasis on quality seasonal ingredients means a constantly changing menu. Indulge your sweet tooth, with homemade apple pie at Winkel 43 (*Noordermarkt 43, 1015 NA*) or head to Buurtboerderij Ons Genoegen (#46) for thick and filling *pannenkoeken* (pancakes). As the first traders to capture the bean market in the 1600s, the Dutch take coffee quite seriously. Try a flat white at any Screaming Beans coffee bars, or a latte at one of de Koffie Salon's five locations.

Be sure to make reservations in advance and note that smaller establishments don't open on Mondays.

Frederik Molenschot
Artist & industrial designer

Hailing from Amsterdam, Molenschot makes objects, art pieces, bronze light sculptures, and sometimes the whole interior. He also collaborates with Carpenters Workshop Gallery.

Vis aan de Schelde
P.070

Fa. Speijkervet
P.071

Sue Doeksen
Visual artist

I'm a visual adventurer born in 1982. My works are overflowing with bright colours, friendly shapes and jokes. Paper-cutting and animations are some of my regular creations.

BCXSY
Multidisciplinary design studio

Set up in 2007 by Boaz Cohen and Sayaka Yamamoto, BCXSY delivers a total experience through the creation and development of concepts, products, graphics and interiors.

De Culinaire Werkplaats
P.072

Monique Goossens
Designer

Playful, humorous and surprising, Goossens's work projects a creative interplay between photography, type and materials. She also lectures at Academie Artemis.

Rijsel
P.073

Wilde Zwijnen
P.074

David Keuning
Editor, MARK

I work at architecture magazine Mark by Frame Publishers. When I am not at work, you can find me running, cycling, rowing on the river Amstel, or sailing on around the city.

Rob van den Nieuwenhuizen
Art director & graphic designer

Also known as "DRAWSWORDS", I teach typography at the Royal Academy of Art in The Hague and the Willem de Kooning Academy. I also work as a creative strategist and copywriter.

Mana Mana
P.075

Scheltens & Abbenes
Photographer & artist duo

Scheltens & Abbenes is combination of still-life photography and creative craftsmanship. Their clients include magazines and cultural institutes in the fashion, design and art field.

Pont 13
P.078

Ewoudt Boonstra
Creative director

Boonstra is from Amsterdam. He has spent his career making commercials, films, books, and art exhibits at creative agencies including KesselsKramer and Wieden+Kennedy Portland.

Vuurtoren-eiland
P.076

Kustaa Saksi
Artist & designer

Finnish-born Saksi does graphic storytelling through patterns, installation and textile art. Combining organic qualities and textures, he explores spaces, objects and atmospheres.

Café Modern
P.080

Floor Nijdeken
Social & product designer

My name is Floor (yes, for real). I work part-time at an architect firm and at times on collaborations. Maybe we'll eat a bitterball together someday in Amsterdam. I just know you will like it!

Mossel & Gin
P.082

Rogier Hendriks
Co-founder, Onesize

I am one of the founders of Amsterdam-based creative studio Onesize. I design, direct, animate, drink and sleep.

Jochem Leegstra
Founder, ...,staat

As ...,staat's creative director, I passionately design for local heroes. I'm addicted to travelling, magazines, espresso and Old Fashioned. Currently living with Julia and our daughter Yuli.

Buurt-boerderij Ons Genoegen
P.081

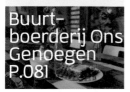

Nacional
P.083

37 Vis aan de Schelde
Map V, P.111

Vis aan de Schelde is an upscale modern dining spot where you'll find meals masterfully and artfully prepared by chef Michiel Deenik. "Seafood and seasons" is the restaurant's theme evidenced by the choice of seafood dishes and a completely new menu every ten weeks. Order the Chef's selection both for the surprise factor and to try the day's freshest catch. Tempt your palate with an exciting mix of seasonal flavour and texture starting from €40 for a three-course meal, tailored to vegetarians and meat eaters alike.

🕐 1200–1430 (M–F), 1730–2300 daily
🏠 Scheldeplein 4, 1078 GR
📞 +31 (0)20 675 1583
URL www.visaandeschelde.nl

"The cook, Michiel Deenik, will give you an unforgettable evening. The interior is created by me and my girl, Esther Stam of Studio Modijefsky!"
– Frederik Molenschot

38 Fa. Speijkervet
Map H, P.107

Head to Speijkervet to enjoy the "new rough" style of restaurant emerging in Amsterdam that aims to recreate the vibe of a grandma's kitchen, where quality, home cooked food is made in a resourceful way. Speijkervet sources their biologically reared products from within 400 km range keeping the food local and organic. They also employs a nose-to-tail approach to their dishes, wasting no ingredients. Whilst the homemade sausages and pork dishes are revered by diners, there are plenty of vegetarian options on the menu.

🕐 1400-0000 (Tu-F), 1100- (Sa-Su)
🏠 Admiraal de Ruijterweg 79, 1057JZ
📞 +31 (0)20 223 6004
URL www.speijkervet.nl

"Their dishes are inspired by the Northern Europeans. The place is always thriving and you can see that everyone is enjoying themselves."

– Sue Doeksen

39 De Culinaire Werkplaats
Map M, P.108

Designed to intersect food and art, you are part of the experience at De Culinaire Werkplaats, seated in the open kitchen and constantly presented with stunning fresh dishes and detailed information about the inspiration behind each one. This intimate vegetarian restaurant experiments with flavours and ideas producing wonderful unexpected creations. The drinks all have a set price, however the menu does not. You decide what you think the meal is worth when it comes to time to pay.

🕐 1830–2230 (F–Sa)
🏠 Fannius Scholtenstraat 10, 1051 EX
📞 +31 (0)65 464 6576
🌐 www.deculinairewerkplaats.nl

"*A new five course meal is introduced each month, featuring all-vegetarian, mainly organic and local ingredients inspired by colours, emotions or plants.*"
– BCXSY

40 Rijsel
Map N, P.109

Owners Pieter Smits and Chef Iwan Driessen
are unapologetic about Rijsel's "no nonsense"
approach to food. The French-Flemish menu
is compact and always changing providing
simple well made food. The attentive staff,
open plan kitchen and white linen-clad tables
create a relaxed atmosphere. Meat is their
speciality, leaving guests raving about the
succulent spring chicken and tender côte de
boeuf. Rijsel's wine list is extensive with classic
choices like Bordeaux to newer varieties like
Loire. Don't hesitate to ask for a good pairing
with your dish.

 1800 till late (M-F)
Marcusstraat 52B, 1091 TK
+31 (0)20 463 2142 rijsel.com

"Very good French kitchen for a fair price."
— Monique Goossens

41 Wilde Zwijnen
Map D, P.105

Rave reviews and great press make Wilde Zwijnen one of the most desirable places to dine. Located in the heart of Indische Buurt, a lively up-and-coming area in the east end of the city Wilde Zwijnen serves quality modern Dutch classics such as fish doused with butter and '*kroketten*' (croquettes) made from regional and seasonal ingredients. Despite the name, Wilde Zwijnen (Dutch for "wild boar"), they also serve vegetarian dishes. The exposed brick interior and hanging plants provide a serene setting for a relaxing meal.

🕐 1200– (F-Su), 1800– daily
🏠 Javaplein 23 hs, 1095 CJ
📞 +31 (0)20 463 3043
URL www.wildezwijnen.com

"Take tram line 14, departing from Dam Square in the city centre. It stops right in front of the door."

– David Keuning, MARK

42 Mana Mana
Map E, P.106

Mana Mana is a small, cosy Israeli vegetarian restaurant with a simple and intriguing concept. For a reasonable fee, enjoy as much food as you wish. A constant stream of delicious and varied homemade vegetarian (or vegan food) is served until you tell the server to stop. This seemingly endless feast lets you try a bit of everything topped off by a single dessert course. Tap water and fresh mint tea are complimentary for the whole evening and wine can be ordered by the bottle.

🕐 1500–0000 (Tu–Su)
🏠 1e Jan Steenstraat 85 hs, 1072 NE
📞 +31 (0)64 163 1098
f manamana Amsterdam

"Eat until you can eat no more."
– Rob van den Nieuwenhuizen aka DRAWSWORDS

43 Vuurtoreneiland
Map K, P.107

Formerly the site of a military fort and home to a three-century old lighthouse – Amsterdam's only one – this island's main attraction is its glass house restaurant. The idyllic natural surroundings provide a charming rustic environment for relishing Dutch fare with French and Mediterranean accents. The four course fixed price meal (excluding drinks) consists of local biological ingredients like meat on the bone and root vegetables prepared using traditional methods of smoking, preserving and roasting and pickling. Hotel facilities are in progress.

🕐 May–Dec 💲 €49.50 🏠 Dock: Veemkade facing Lloyd Hotel (#3) 📞 +31 (0)61 558 3838
🔠 www.vuurtoreneiland.nl 🔗 Experience lasts 5 hours (incl. 90–120 min round trip). Boat leaves at 1830 (W–Sa), 1530 (Su). Prior booking up to 2 months. No refund. Limited tickets sell on the day. Children's menu are offered on Sundays at a reduced price.

"Go to this deserted island for an intimate dinner night in a glass house, you won't even think you are at the outskirts of Amsterdam."

– Scheltens & Abbenes

44 Pont 13
Map Q, P.111

Off the beaten path is this quaint restaurant in a converted 1920s ferry boat serving reasonably priced quality food. The menu features family style dishes including a variety of fresh sustainably sourced seafood options such as half a lobster and whole grilled fish prepared to perfection. All side dishes are served separately to mains and offer unique flavour combinations. The chef sources the charcuterie products from Italy, including a whole salami range. Interestingly, everything you see inside is for sale, including furniture so don't shy from asking for a price.

🕐 1200–2200 daily 🏠 Haparandadam 50, 1013 AK
📞 +31 (0)20 770 2722 🔳 www.pont13.nl
✐ *Restaurant may be closed for private parties, or on selected days during the winter season.*

"*Its smoky, authentic interior fits very well with superb French/Dutch cuisine. It's a cosy place to stay when the weather gets tough. They have the best boat dog too!*"
– Kustaa Saksi

45 Café Modern
Map L, P.108

The culinary creativity at Café Modern is for anyone with an adventurous or curious palate. The fixed price five-course mystery dinner menu changes weekly and only reveals limited ingredients per course, creating an element of surprise. Located in the hipster area of Van der Pekbuurt, restauranteur Niels Wouters, who also runs Hotel de Goudfazant, is known for creating foodie destinations. Café Modern is also home to Sweet Dreamz, a boutique hotel above the restaurant. During the day, the café is leased out to Jacques Jour which serves breakfast and lunch.

🕐 1900–0000 (M–Sa)
🏠 Meidoornweg 2, 1031 GG 📞 +31 (0)20 494 0684
URL www.modernamsterdam.nl

"Take a free ferry across IJ to get there. The café resides in an old bank building in Amsterdam Noord. The interior has a classic Dutch 1950s vibe and the food is superb."

– Ewoudt Boonstra

46 Buurtboerderij Ons Genoegen

Map S, P.111

Well hidden by trees, flowering meadows and grazing sheep, it's understandable why Buurtboerderij Ons Genoegen is coveted by locals. This beautiful public farm is an urban retreat that serves hearty soups, deli-sandwiches and homemade cakes at its cafe. Definitely try the pancakes. All food is prepared by a dedicated team of volunteers who donate their time to keep the farm in tip top shape. By eating here you support the farm and all of its activities including craft workshops, educational classes and a second hand shop.

🕐 1000-2200 (M-Th), -0000 (F), 1100- (Sa-Su)
🏠 Spaarndammerdijk 319, 1014 AA
📞 +31 (0)20 337 6820 🌐 www.buurtboerderij.nl

"Perhaps people are going to hate me for giving you this tip and maybe it's an undiscovered gem for tourists."

– Floor Nijdeken

 47 Mossel & Gin
Map M, P.108

The core concept for Mossel & Gin, as the name
suggests, is mussels and gin. Expert pairings of
various species of mussels cooked in a French,
Asian, or Dutch fusion style, combined with
inventive gin based cocktails will leave your
tastebuds invigorated. The prevailing presence
of gin is evident not only in their drinks list
but also in the food like their "ginmayo". The
restaurant is close to Westergasfabriek, where
NeighbourFood Market takes place on the third
Sunday of every month from 11am to 6pm.

🕐 1700–0100 (Tu–Sa), 1300– (Su)
🏠 Gosschalklaan 12, 1014 DC
📞 +31 (0)20 486 5869 🔗 www.mosselengin.nl

"*If you like mussels, go here. Great location,
good food, good atmosphere. Kallenbach Gallery
(Pazzanistraat 9–11) is just nearby.*"

– Rogier Hendriks, Onesize

48 Nacional

Map A, P.102

Nacional is serial restaurateur Casper Reinders' newest venture located in Amsterdam's city centre near Leidseplein. The French bistro with a modern New York twist serves breakfast lunch and dinner, offering all the classic French staples, including onion soup, steak tartare, duck confit and salad niçoise, prepared masterfully. The wine list is expansive so don't be shy in asking the knowledgeable staff for recommendations. If you don't have time for dinner, pop in for breakfast or lunch between 10am and 4pm and enjoy a Mimosa or Bellini.

🕐 1000–2300 (Su–Th), –0000 (F–Sa)
🏠 Kleine-Gartmanplantsoen 11A, 1017 RP
📞 +31 (0)20 205 0908 　URL　 nacional.nl

"Think vintage pieces combined with a Parra sculpture.
P.S. my bonus hidden gem for the best cocktails is
Hiding in Plain Sight (Papenburg 18, 1011 TX)."

– Jochem Leegstra, ...,staat

Nightlife

Cozy hideouts, arcade game night, cultural fetes and meet

It is not just the red light district will offer you the Amsterdam style night entertainment. The real party scene is actually far away from the tourist culture most people recognise.

Most bars boast the best views of Amsterdam at sunset. Truth be told, with such an abundance you'll enjoy stunning views from just about any patio, barge, rooftop or theatre. Bars like Bimhuis (#54) and IJ-Kantine (*Mt. Ondinaweg 15-17, 1033 RE*) offer chic environments and gorgeous vistas of the water of IJ. For a relaxed vibe, the Westerpark area is full of places to sit and drink.

You won't feel pressure to conform in Amsterdam. Have a quiet night with a glass of wine or one that begins with video games in TonTon Club (#57). If you have the stamina for an all-nighter, party in Doka at the basement of Volkshotel (#56) or watch the sunrise from Pacific Parc. Avoid taking taxis as the fares are steep and they often take unnecessary detours. Also walk with confidence and company at night to avoid unsolicited offers. Lucky for the gents, although wilding peeing is forbidden, there are designated open air public urinals available, called *Krul*. Ladies prepare to pay for every visit to the toilet, because it is a mission to find a public toilet that doesn't charge you, even fast food chains!

Anne Barlinckhoff
Photographer

I have a deep love for this planet and everything on it. I like photographing females, animals and nature, even better when all combines! Bananas are my favourite fruit.

Door 74
P.088

Tolhuistuin
P.089

Andre Maat
Film director

I direct commercials, music videos, animations and everything in between. I love Amsterdam for my daily bike and ferry rides and its small size yet big ambitions.

Loes Faber
Illustrator & visual artist

Hi! I've been living in Amsterdam for about three years now. Besides my creative work I also teach at Academie Minerva. I love to draw for days and drinks with my friends at rooftops.

De Trut
P.090

Jeroen Vester
Founder, Ninetynine

Founder of Ninetynine, an interior design studio that works on hospitality, retail and office design. Coffeecompany, East57 and VICE Benelux Headquarter are among his projects.

Bar Mash
P.091

De Nieuwe
Anita
P.092

Marta Veludo
Art director & graphic designer

Amsterdam is where I work, live and love. Digitally or tangibly, I combine disciplines with visual identities, fashion, and motion design for both cultural and commercial fields.

Hagar Vardimon
Artist & designer

Also known as Happy Red Fish, I work with photographs and threads, love taking pictures, collecting vintage books and toys. I have a soft spot for quirky little things.

Bimhuis
P.094

NOMAN
Display & set design studio

Founded by Selina Parr (fashion) and Lara Tolman (product), NOMAN creates installations and films. Their work appeared at Design Week Beijing 2013 and DEPOT BASEL among others.

Noam Erlich
Executive producer, ACHTUNG!

I'm executive producer at creative agency ACHTUNG! and launched Kraftwerk, a sub-label which provides design driven solutions. I love to work with passionate talented people.

Jeroen Krielaars
Motion director & designer

Jeroen Krielaars leads Calango, a small design studio from the heart of Amsterdam that works on projects at the intersection of direction, graphic design and motion design since 2006.

Marcel Vrieswijk
Partner, PlusOne

Resident of the beautiful city of Amsterdam and partner/managing director of design and animation studio PlusOne. Loving food and music along the way.

Joseph Burrin
Design director, Wieden+Kennedy

I have lived here for four years with my family. I design Printed Pages. In the little spare time I have I enterain with record label projects Keyboard Masher & Pleasure Unit.

Mattijs de Wit
Graphic designer

Mattijs de Wit has been working for a wide range of clients in the cultural and commercial field since 2002. He is an independent designer and co-founded studio OK200.

49 **Door 74**
Map A, P.103

Netherland's first speakeasy style bar honours the 1920s prohibition-era need for secrecy by keeping its location hidden. To ensure no paper trail, reservations can only be made over the phone on the day. Once you arrive there is no indication that you're in the right place, aside from a window with a doorbell. The secrecy is worth it for the dimly lit, sultry ambience with sensational cocktail creations. Whilst the cocktails are pricey, the quality concoctions and the atmosphere justify the cost. Consult their facebook page before you go for important house rules.

🕐 2000-0300 (Su-Th), -0400 (F-Sa)
🏠 Reguliersdwarsstraat 74I, 1017 BN
📞 +31 (0)63 404 5122 [URL] www.door-74.com

"I miss the peanut butter jelly cocktail! Look for the darkest colour black door in the Reguliersdwarsstraat."

– Anne Barlinckhoff

50 Tolhuistuin

Map L, P.108

Minutes from Central station, in Amsterdam Noord, the former offices of Shell Oil have been made over for all kinds of evening entertainment. Now known as Tolhuistuin, the cultural destination hosts events from dance and visual arts, to music programmes run by the famous Paradiso club. There's also a bar and restaurant THT with panoramic views of the IJ. For a relaxed night, tuck into a plate of nachos and stroll around the labyrinth of paths in the park after dusk or sit around the firepit. For something livelier, check out the lineup of DJs and festivals which run from 11pm until 6am.

🕐 1000–0100 daily 🏠 IJpromenade 2, 1031 KT
📞 +31 (0)20 760 4820 🌐 www.tolhuistuin.nl

"Tolhuistuin has it all: a garden, concerts, art, and other cultural events. The film museum is just a few minutes walk away."

– Andre Maat

51 De Trut
Map C, P.105

Founded in the mid-80s, this popular Sunday night disco spot emerged as a result of a regular gathering of the LGBTQ community for discos in the basement of a former squat. The ethos of the club is good music, good atmosphere and affordable prices in a safe, fun and accepting space. The club runs as a social venture, where all staff are voluntary and surplus profits go to support the LGBTQ community through HIV/AIDS projects around the world. The capacity is only 220 people so arrive early to avoid disappointment.

🕐 2300–0300 (Su) **S** price vary with parties
🏠 Bilderdijkstraat 165–E, 1053 KP
📞 +31 (0)20 612 3524
URL www.trutfonds.nl 📎 18+

"*The 'Trut' is a really nice club for the LGBTQ community, it's only open on Sunday night. Make sure you're in the queue before ten!*"

– Loes Faber

52 Bar Mash
Map E, P.106

Blink and you might miss Bar Mash. At 35 square metres, it's one of the tiniest bars in town. Once inside, enter a world of plywood furniture, long tables and an ever-evolving selection of gin, beer and bar snacks. The team behind the bar are constantly looking to find the best products to enhance their offering. The atmosphere invites all crowds which you can see spilling out onto Gerard Douplein square. Studio Ninetynine is to be credited for the warm decor inside.

🕐 1400–0100 daily
🏠 Gerard Douplein 9, 1073 XE
📞 +31 (0)20 664 4428

"When you're there, make sure to ask for their homemade Finocchietto."

– Jeroen Vester, Ninetynine

 *Showtime & price vary with programmes*
Frederik Hendrikstraat 111, 1052 HN
URL *www.denieuweanita.nl*

53 De Nieuwe Anita
Map I, P.107

De Nieuwe Anita is one of the best alternative venues in town, an environment that is a cross between a comfortable living room and an x-rated movie theatre, with vintage inspired interiors consisting of old lampshades and flowery sofas. There's a small bar with food, movie screenings, theatre performances, live music and dancing. Each night has a different agenda which never fails to entertain and inspire. Vegetarian restaurant Robin Food is in the same building and on Monday nights you can get a €1 ticket for the movie screening when you order food.

"From concerts behind the counter to Mexican night and haircuts sessions, the cosy and homey feeling makes it the best dance floor in town."
– Marta Veludo

54 Bimhuis
Map P, P.110

Highly acclaimed as one of the best jazz concert venues in the world, Bimhuis supplies stunning views of IJ from its upstairs café and an unpretentious environment to enjoy jazz and experimental music. Charles Mingus, Chet Baker, Archie Shepp are amongst the great musicians to have ever been in the club's lineup. On the first Monday of each month, a music and dance impro lab explores the inter-action of sound, movement, light and space. Every Tuesday night (except in July and August) there's an open improvisational workshop.

🕐 1830–0100 (Su–Th), –0300 (F–Sa)
💲 Ticket price varies with programmes
🏠 Piet Heinkade 3, 1019 BR 📞 +31 (0)20 788 2188
URL bimhuis.com

"Nice restaurant, very nice bar."

– Hagar Vardimon aka Happy Red Fish

55 Wynand Fockink

Map A P.103

Since the 17th century, Wynand Fockink has been specialising in liqueurs and jenevers (a Dutch gin), which they still make in their own distillery. They still use the pot and method from 300 some years ago to create that distinctive authentic flavour and depth. Wynand Fockink's quaint tasting room stocks an impressive selection of their house specialties to be tasted from a brimful little glass. Bent and take a sip before picking up the glass! The room can only accept seven people top at a time so be sure to register if you wish to join their Saturday tasting.

🕐 Tasting room: 1500–2100 daily, store: 1500–2100 (Su–Th), 1200– (F–Sa) 🏠 Pijlsteeg 31, 1012 HH
📞 +31 (0)20 639 2695 🔗 www.wynand-fockink.nl
🖊 Tasting workshop: €17.50 per head, 1–5 persons: 1400 (Sa), Booking required.

"Go for local liquor, and get really drunk."

– Selina Parr & Lara Tolman, NOMAN

 56 **Volkshotel**
Map N, P.109

Volkshotel has something for everyone. Converted from newspaper *De Volkskrant*'s former
offices, this new hotel integrates a restaurant,
affordable accommodation, creative work
spaces and an exuberant nightlife scene. Volkshotel is trendy, boasting a unique decor and
hosting interactive art displays, talk shows and
a full agenda of events – day and night. Grab
dinner, a cocktail or go clubbing at Canvas, the
hotel's rooftop bar with panoramic views of
the city and a lineup of discos, music launch
parties and sets by stellar DJs. Its basement
hideout hosts an obscure cocktail bar, Doka.

🕐 *Canvas: 0700-0100 (M-Th), –0400 (F), 0800-
0400 (Sa), 0800– (Su)* 🏠 *Wibautstraat 150, 1091 GR*
URL *www.volkshotel.nl* 🔗 *Cover charge applies
to Canvas club nights: 2200-0400 (F-Sa)*

"*Volkshotel is a lot of things. A hotel, bar and
restaurant, all to be found on different floors.*"
– Noam Erlich, ACHTUNG!

 57 TonTon Club
Map B, P.105

Set your inner child free at TonTon Club, a very
cool arcade hall containing all the best games
from yesteryear. Relive your Mortal Combat
prowess whilst drinking great beer or chow
down on a hotdog between rounds of air
hockey. Founded by four young men through a
crowdfunding campaign, play is the main aim
of this establishment where you can enjoy old
school board games, 3D printers, and experimental games like a pinball drawing machine.
Closing time is midnight so make this the first
stop on your night out.

 ⏰ 1600–0000 (M–Tu), 1200–0015
(W–Su) 🏠 Sint Annendwarsstraat
6, 1012 HC 🌐 www.tontonclub.nl

"Visit this arcade in the middle of the red light district
for an old street fighter match against your friends."
– Jeroen Krielaars, Calango

 58 **Bar Oldenhof**
Map A, P.102

Bar Oldenhof is a relaxed, old fashioned establishment that encourages a slower pace of life. A quaint interior with cozy chairs and a civilised crowd provides a calming ambience, like you've travelled back in time. Run by the Oldenhof brothers, Dwight and Quinz, the bar has a fantastic wide range of whiskies. Sip on a single Scottish malt or ask the Oldenhof's for a recommendation. It has a no reservations policy so can just turn up.

 1900–0100 (Tu–Th), –0300 (F–Sa)
Elandsgracht 84, 1016 TZ
URL www.bar-oldenhof.com

"Once inside you'll be overwhelmed by the prestige, yet cozy and easy going layout."
– Marcel Vrieswijk, PlusOne

59 Roest

Map J, P.107

Run by the same creative collection as Canvas and Doka, Roest (Dutch for "rust") exudes a vibrant and inviting atmosphere though several indoor and outdoor venues. In the summer there's an urban beach that evolves into a street party and in the winter there's a big fire place. Enjoy a drink at the bar or eat at a food stall before watching a gig at this creative haven for art, theatre, film and music. Vrijland Festival returns to Roest on Liberation Day with DJs veering from techno and house to soul and funk.

🕐 1600–0000 (W), –0100 (Th), –0300 (F), 1100–0300 (Sa), 1100– (Su) 🏠 Jacob Bontiusplaats 1, 1018 PL
📞 +31 (0)20 308 0283 URL www.amsterdamroest.nl

"I like drinking out at Café Westerdok for crazy random booze ups, then Red Light Radio parties are fun. Roest can be well worth a visit depending what's on."

– Joseph Burrin, Wieden+Kennedy.

60 Basis
Map N, P.109

A great selection of beer, wines and spirits and weekly programme of cultural events are reason enough to check out Basis, but its 'Bring Your Own Food' concept is the main attraction of the one of a kind bar. Basis provides plates, cutlery, ovens, microwaves - everything you need to enjoy your food and they even do the dishes after. The owners extend the bring-your-own sentiment to people's ideas and creativity, inviting anyone to exhibit work, perform or collaborate on future projects.

🕐 1600–0000 (Su-Th), –0300 (F-Sa)
🏠 Tolstraat 182, 1074 VM
URL www.basisamsterdam.nl

"The crowd is a good mix of locals, backpackers and tourists. Always a good relaxed atmosphere with weekly and irregular programmes like art exhibitions and such."

– Mattijs de Wit

DISTRICT MAP : **JORDAAN, GRACHTENGORDEL-WEST, DE WETERINGSCHANS**

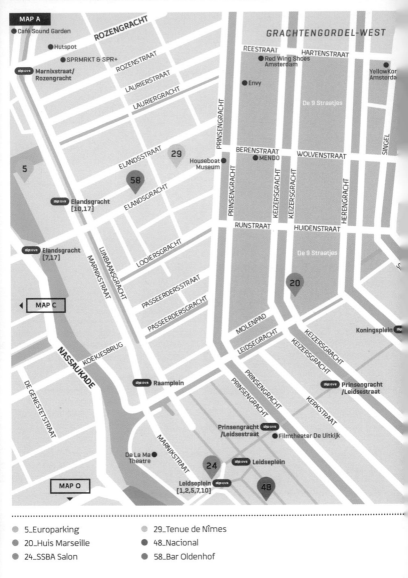

- 5_Europarking
- 20_Huis Marseille
- 24_SSBA Salon
- 29_Tenue de Nîmes
- 48_Nacional
- 58_Bar Oldenhof

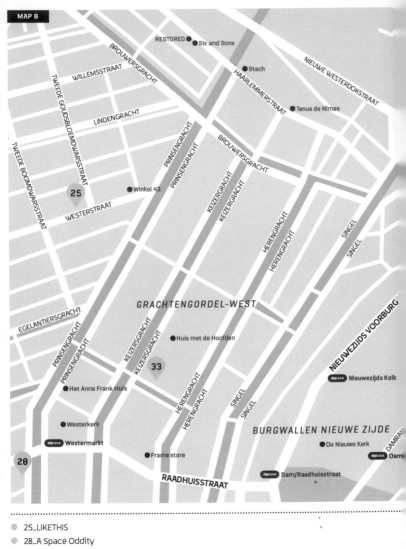

MAP B

- 25_LIKETHIS
- 28_A Space Oddity
- 33_Architectura & Natura

- 9_Amsterdam Centraal
- 16_Eddie the Eagle Museum
- 17_Ons' Lieve Heer op Solder
- 18_P/////AKT
- 31_San Serriffe
- 34_De Hallen Amsterdam
- 41_Wilde Zwijnen
- 51_De Trut
- 57_TonTon Club

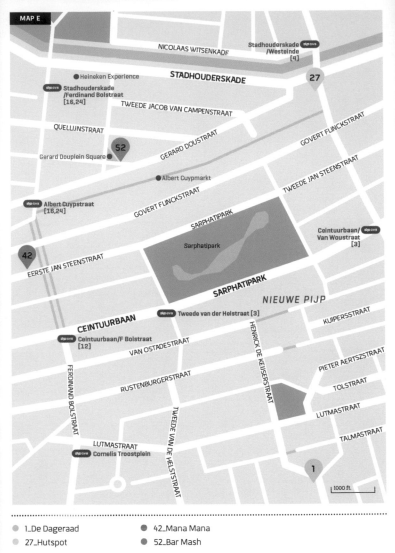

- 1_De Dageraad
- 27_Hutspot
- 42_Mana Mana
- 52_Bar Mash

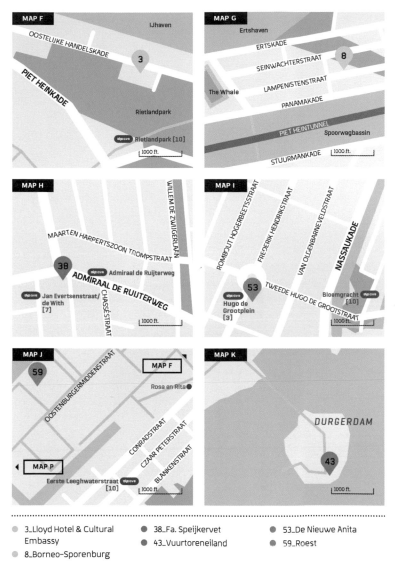

- 3_Lloyd Hotel & Cultural Embassy
- 8_Borneo-Sporenburg
- 38_Fa. Speijkervet
- 43_Vuurtoreneiland
- 53_De Nieuwe Anita
- 59_Roest

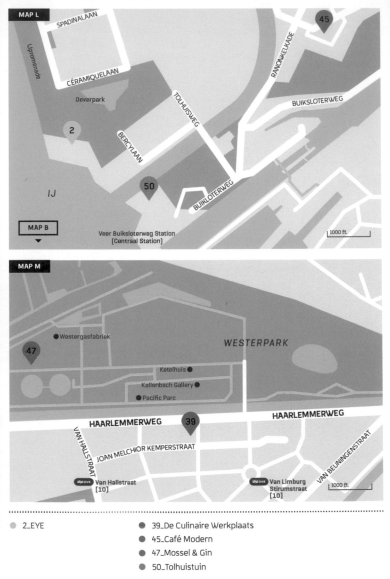

● 2_EYE

● 39_De Culinaire Werkplaats

● 45_Café Modern

● 47_Mossel & Gin

● 50_Tolhuistuin

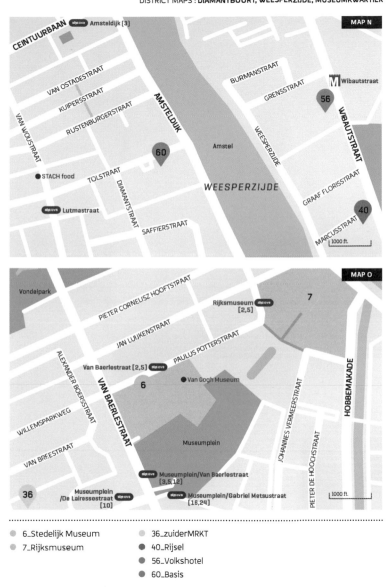

- 6_Stedelijk Museum
- 7_Rijksmuseum
- 36_zuiderMRKT
- 40_Rijsel
- 56_Volkshotel
- 60_Basis

DISTRICT MAP : **NIEUWMARKT EN LASTAGE, OOSTERDOKSEILAND, EASTERN DOCKLANDS**

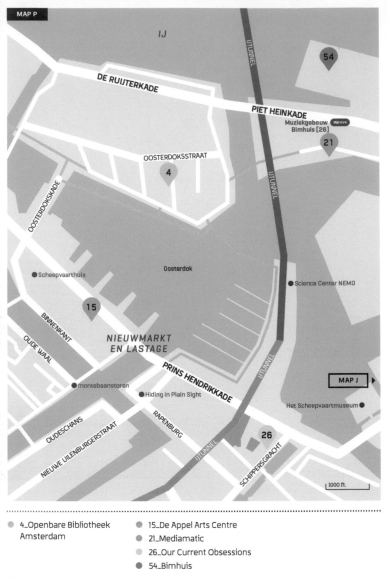

MAP P

IJ

UTUNNEL

DE RUIJTERKADE

PIET HEINKADE

54

Muziekgebouw
Bimhuis [26]

21

OOSTERDOKSSTRAAT

4

OOSTERDOKSKADE

Oosterdok

● Scheepvaarthuis

● Science Center NEMO

15

BINNENKANT

OUDE WAAL

*NIEUWMARKT
EN LASTAGE*

PRINS HENDRIKKADE

● montebaanstoren

● Hiding in Plain Sight

MAP J ▶

UTUNNEL

Het Scheepvaartmuseum ●

OUDESCHANS

NIEUWE UILENBURGERSTRAAT

RAPENBURG

26

SCHIPPERSGRACHT

UTUNNEL

1000 ft.

● 4_Openbare Bibliotheek
    Amsterdam

● 15_De Appel Arts Centre

● 21_Mediamatic

● 26_Our Current Obsessions

● 54_Bimhuis

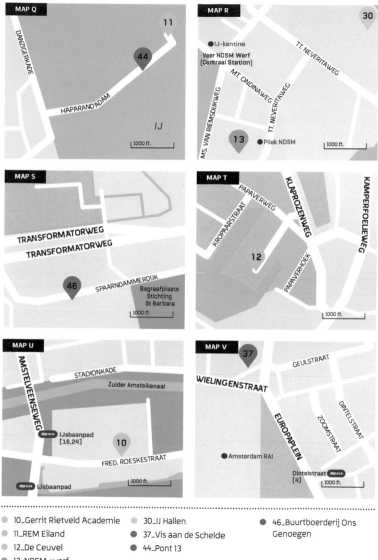

- 10_Gerrit Rietveld Academie
- 11_REM Eiland
- 12_De Ceuvel
- 13_NDSM-werf
- 30_IJ Hallen
- 37_Vis aan de Schelde
- 44_Pont 13
- 46_Buurtboerderij Ons Genoegen

Accommodations

Hip hostels, fully-equipped apartments & swanky hotels

No journey is perfect without a good night's sleep to recharge. Whether you're backpacking or on a business trip, our picks combine top quality and convenience, whatever your budget.

 $** < €80   **$$** €81–200   **$$$ €201+

Hotel Not Hotel

Comfort is not compromised here, despite its topsy-turvy setting. Check in for a brief respite from the outside world and jump into this space where guests stay in rooms hidden behind bookcases, in tram carts, and a cottage fully committed to its printed theme. Seven of them come with private shower or bathrooms. Great vibe and bike hire are always on-site.

🏠 *Piri Reisplein 34, 1057 KH*
🕐 *+31 (0)20 820 4538* **URL** *hotelnothotel.com* **$$**

Volkshotel

With creative studios, a swarming club, and a calendar full of festivals and parties, Volkshotel is where life happens 24/7. Stylishly simple rooms by local designer Bas van Tol and nine special rooms accommodate up to four. Rooftop sauna and hot tubs are to be enjoyed with a gorgeous panoramic view of the city.

🏠 *Wibautstraat 150, 1091 GR*
📞 *+31 (0)20 261 2100* URL *volkshotel.nl*

The Conservatorium

World-class museums are on this hotel's door-step. Housed in a splendid 1900s bank building, the Conservatorium offers class service with 129 lofty rooms, each complimented with a spacious bathroom, a personal host and access to their 1,000 sqm gym and spa. Begin your day with a run at the nearby Vondelpark.

🏠 *Van Baerlestraat 27, 1071 AN* 📞 *+31 (0)20 570 0000* URL *conservatoriumhotel.com* 💲

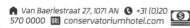

Hotel IX Amsterdam

🏠 *Hartenstraat 8, 1016 CB*
📞 *+31 (0)20 845 8451*
URL *www.hotelixamsterdam.com*

Lloyd Hotel

🏠 *Oostelijke Handelskade 34, 1019 BN*
📞 *+31 (0)20 561 3636*
URL *www.lloydhotel.com*

The Dylan

🏠 *Keizersgracht 384, 1016 GB*
📞 *+31 (0)20 530 2010*
URL *www.dylanamsterdam.com*

Notes

Index

–

In Accommodation: all courtesy
of respective hotels.

CITIX60

CITIx60: Amsterdam

First published and distributed by
viction workshop ltd

viction:ary™

7C Seabright Plaza, 9-23 Shell Street,
North Point, Hong Kong

Url: www.victionary.com
Email: we@victionary.com
🄵 www.facebook.com/victionworkshop
🐦 www.twitter.com/victionary_
🌐 www.weibo.com/victionary

Edited and produced by viction:ary

Concept & art direction: Victor Cheung
Research & editorial: Queenie Ho, Jovan Lip, Eunyi Choi
Project coordination: Katherine Wong, Jovan Lip
Design & map illustration: Frank Lo

Contributing writer: Katee Hui
Cover map illustration: Stefan Glerum
Count to 10 illustrations: Guillaume Kashima aka Funny Fun
Photography: Sofia Garefi

Content is compiled based on facts available as of February 2015. Travellers
are advised to check for updates from respective locations before your visit.

First edition
ISBN 978-988-13203-1-5
Printed and bound in China

Acknowledgements

A special thank you to all creatives, photographer(s), editor, producers, com-
panies and organisations for your crucial contributions to our inspiration and
knowledge necessary for the creation of this book. And, to the many whose
names are not credited but have participated in the completion of the book,
we thank you for your input and continuous support all along.

CITIX60
City Guides

CITIx60 is a handpicked list of hot spots that illustrates the spirit of the world's most exhilarating design hubs. From what you see to where you stay, this city guide series leads you to experience the best — the places that only passionate insiders know and go.

Each volume is a unique collaboration with local creatives from selected cities. Known for their accomplishments in fields as varied as advertising, architecture and graphics, fashion, industry and food, music and publishing, these locals are at the cutting edge of what's on and when. Whether it's a one-day stopover or a longer trip, **CITIx60** is your inspirational guide.

Stay tuned for new editions.

City guides available now:

Amsterdam
Barcelona
Berlin
Hong Kong
London
Los Angeles
New York
Paris
Tokyo